HEALING
RELATIONSHIPS
THROUGH FORGIVENESS

*DISPLAYING GOD'S GRACE
TO OTHERS*

A WORKBOOK COMPANION
FOR GROUP STUDY
PART 3

DONALD E. JONES, PHD

J & A BOOK PUBLISHERS
www.jabookpublishers.com

ISBN-10:1-946368-01-6
ISBN-13:978-1-946368-01-0

DEDICATION

I dedicate this book to my Savior and Lord Jesus Christ. He has been with me every step of my journey upon the earth, and I so look forward to being in His presence forever and ever.

CONTENTS

ACKNOWLEDGMENTS

I want to thank my wonderful and gracious wife Carol who has supported me in this ministry with sacrifice, enthusiasm, encouragement, and accountability. Most of all, she has been a constant blessing because of her willingness to listen. I was always sharing with her the truths God had been teaching me as I studied His word and wrote this book. It consumed many hours. Thank you, Carol, and I deeply love you.

I want to thank my son Gregory R. Jones for volunteering to be the primary editor of this important book. Without his time and effort in painstakingly and meticulously going over every word and every sentence checking and rechecking the sentence structure and grammar, I would not have been able to complete it. Thank you for your ministry to me. I love you my son.

I want to thank my other children, Krista, Matt, and Kara for their love for Christ and His Word and their willingness to live for Him. I love you all.

Introduction

This workbook is designed to aid in the comprehension and application of the truths from the Scriptures which are found in the book of the same name. It has a question and answer format because asking questions was a powerful teaching method that the Lord used to reveal God's divine truth. Jesus asked over one hundred and thirty questions as He instructed the people of God and others. These are only the recorded ones. We can only speculate as to how many questions He might have actually asked. The Lord used His questioning techniques to prompt His listeners to focus, understand, analyze, evaluate, and apply the principles He was proclaiming to them. The same has been done in this workbook.

In Luke chapter 24, the Lord had already resurrected but had only appeared to the women who had gone to His tomb. Many of His followers did not understand why Jesus had died. He was supposed to be the Savior and now He was gone. Two on the road to Emmaus (Cleopas and another) were traveling to the town and discussing this perplexing state of affairs when Jesus appeared. Luke states that their eyes were supernaturally prevented from recognizing Him. The Lord approached them and inquired as to what they were discussing. Here Jesus uses a question to draw out the information He needs to provide the context for His time of instruction. Cleopas could not believe what he had asked. It was all anyone was talking about. He asked Jesus why He did not know the thing that had just occurred in Jerusalem. In verse 19, Luke describes the Lord's simple response, "He said to them, 'What things?'" Our Savior utilizes another question to get to crux of what they knew. This was not for His sake (since He knew their minds) but to display their ignorance of the Scriptures and its prophecies of Him.

1

The two men explained that a prophet named Jesus from Nazareth who had done miraculous deeds was killed by the chief priests. They had hoped that He would redeem Israel. The women who had gone to His tomb claimed that angels had appeared and His body was gone. Yet, it had been three days of silence and they were discouraged. The veiled Lord responds with a strong rebuke and another key question. In verse 25-26, the apostle writes, "He said to them, 'Foolish men, and slow of heart to believe in all that the prophets have spoken! Didn't the Christ have to suffer these things and to enter into his glory?'"

Here again, the Messiah asks a rhetorical question. This time it is to assist them in understanding the connection between Jesus of Nazareth and the words of the prophets. Without waiting for an answer, the Lord launches into His teaching concerning all the Messianic prophecies and other truths about Him in the Scriptures. He stayed with them that night. As they were having a meal together, the traveler's eyes were opened and they saw that it was Jesus who had been speaking to them the entire time. Then, Christ vanished into thin air. Each looked at the other and described how their hearts were burning inside of them as Jesus spoke of Himself in all the Scriptures. As Jesus used questions, so shall we. May these questions help you focus, understand, analyze, evaluate, and apply these critical biblical principles.

Chapter 1

Forgive as Forgiven

If others sin against us in a relationship, we must forgive them as God forgives us. This applies to any and all sins over the course of the relationship.

In the section, "A Typical Scenario," the author describes a co-worker stealing a Christian's idea and his unwillingness to forgive which will need reconciliation.

What is the scenario about?

What did the conflict concern?

What was the relationship between the parties?

Have you had a similar experience?

In the section, "A Scriptural Principle" the author presents an important biblical principle in the forgiveness process which concerns forgiving as we are forgiven.

How would you express this principle in your own words?

How would you rewrite this principle to make it even more personal to your life (using your name and situation)?

Why do you think this principle might be important in your life right now?

How would you rate yourself on the percentage of times you followed this principle in the past when you did something wrong in a relationship?

Directions: Put a horizontal mark and your name where you see yourself on the percentage line.

| 0% | 25% | 50% | 75% | 100% |

In the section, "A Biblical Explanation," the author explains the reasons why we are to forgive as we are forgiven and how to do it.

How do we sometimes make distinctions among people in our forgiveness?

According to Mark 11:25 and Luke 11:4, what key words are used by the Lord Jesus to demonstrate that all people should be forgiven whether they are believers are unbelievers?

To aid in our forgiveness process, what kind of comparison should we make concerning our own sins with the sins of those against us?

If Christians are having a difficult time of forgiving people, what might they not be doing enough of?

Is the forgiveness of others dependent on their response to us? Why or why not?

In what ways might these truths impact your relationships?

In the section, "An Ancient Portrait," the author presents the parable of the servant who was unwilling to forgive.

What was the king's response to his servant's plea?

What was the first servant's response to the second servant's plea?

How were the two responses different from each other and why?

What actions did the king take when he found out?

According to this parable of Jesus why should we forgive as forgiven?

Have you ever been in a situation comparable to the king or either servant's dilemma? How was it different or the same?

In the section, "A Modern Anecdote," the author discusses a situation in which a young lady struggled with forgiving her father.

Why did the young lady come in for counseling?

Why was the young lady bitter toward her father?

Rather than confront her father, what did she do?

How did the young lady misinterpret her father's behavior toward her mother?

Why did she not want to forgive her father?

Based on the truths learned in this chapter, what would you have done differently if you were the bitter daughter, the unknowing father, or the traditional mother?

In the section, "A Personal Response," the author provides a model you may use for prayer if you find it necessary after discovering the truths in this chapter.

Are you presently in a relationship where you have sinned against another and have not asked God for forgiveness? If not, is there one from the past that still needs this prayer to be prayed?

Based on the truths you have just learned, what will you continue doing in your current relationships and what will you do differently?

What additional thoughts would you like to share with the others?

Chapter 2

Forgive the Forgiven

When Christians struggle with forgiving other Christians who have hurt them, they should remember that God has already forgiven those very sins on the cross.

In the section, "A Typical Scenario," the author describes an angry encounter between friends which needed restoration.

What is the scenario about?

What did the conflict concern?

What was the relationship between the parties?

Have you had a similar experience?

In the section, "A Scriptural Principle" the author presents an important biblical principle in the forgiveness process which concerns forgiving the forgiven.

How would you express this principle in your own words?

How would you rewrite this principle to make it even more personal to your life (using your name and situation)?

Why do you think this principle might be important in your life right now?

How would you rate yourself on the percentage of times you followed this principle in the past when you did something wrong in a relationship?

Directions: Put a horizontal mark and your name where you are on the percentage line.

0%   25%   50%   75%   100%

In the section, "A Biblical Explanation," the author explains the many reasons why we are to forgive believers who have already been forgiven by God and how to do it.

How does the Lord God's forgiveness of our sins pertain to his forgiveness of other sins against us?

According to Luke 17:3-4, is there a limit on the number of times we should forgive?

According to Matthew 26:28, what does the blood of Christ do to the sins that are committed against us by believers?

According to 1 Timothy 1:15-17, how was Paul, the apostle, the Lord's classical example of forgiveness?

Why was it so difficult for Paul to be forgiven and accepted by Christians?

In what ways might these truths impact your relationships?

In the section, "An Ancient Portrait," the author describes the parable of the Prodigal Son from the perspective of the older brother who did not want to forgive.

How did the father show the younger brother his love and forgiveness when he returned?

How did the older brother want the father to demonstrate his love to him?

Do you think the older brother loved his father and younger brother and how do you know?

What did the older brother want the father to do to the younger brother instead?

What were the three reasons why the older brother would not forgive the younger brother for what he had done?

Have you ever been in a situation comparable to the older brother who had difficulty forgiving or the father who had to handle it? How was it different and how was it the same?

In the section, "A Modern Anecdote," the author explains a son's struggle to forgive his mother who had come to Christ.

What were the three ways in which the mother traumatized the young man and his siblings growing up?

How did the man attempt to help his mother as a child?

How did the man deal with his mother once he had become an adult?

When the mother came to Christ, why did the man still have difficulty forgiving her?

What was biblical truth that caused the man to change his mind and finally forgive his mother for what she done?

Based on the truths learned in this chapter, what would you have done differently if you were the mother who neglected her children or the man who was neglected?

In the section, "A Personal Response," the author provides a model you may use for prayer if you find it necessary after discovering the truths in this chapter.

Are you presently in a relationship where you have sinned against another and have not asked God for forgiveness? If not, is there one from the past that still needs this prayer to be prayed?

Based on the truths you have just learned, what will you continue doing in your current relationships and what will you do differently?

What additional thoughts would you like to share with the others?

Chapter 3

Forgive the Lost

If Christians have difficulty with forgiving those who do not know Christ, they should see them as lost in desperate need of salvation rather than as wicked in need of judgment.

In the section, "A Typical Scenario," the author contrasts the reaction of a husband with his wife's toward the mistakes of a neighbor.

What is the scenario about?

What did the conflict concern?

What was the relationship between the parties?

Have you had a similar experience?

In the section, "A Scriptural Principle" the author presents an important biblical principle in the forgiveness process which concerns viewing unbelievers as lost rather than wicked.

How would you express this principle in your own words?

How would you rewrite this principle to make it even more personal to your life (using your name and situation)?

Why do you think this principle might be important in your life right now?

How would you rate yourself on the percentage of times you followed this principle in the past when you did something wrong in a relationship?

Directions: Put a horizontal mark and your name where you are on the percentage line.

| 0% | 25% | 50% | 75% | 100% |

In the section, "A Biblical Explanation," the author explains the reasons why we are to view unbelievers as lost in order to forgive them and how to do it.

In Luke 9:51–56, what did James and John want to do to the Samaritan village for rejecting Jesus and what was the Lord's response?

How is the concept of man being lost and blind related?

If those who sin against us receive Christ, what will happen to those sins?

What are two groups who participated in Christ's crucifixion and how did He view them in order to forgive them?

Though Christ asked God, the Father, to forgive them, could they be forgiven without receiving Christ? Why or why not?

In what ways might these truths impact your relationships?

In the section, "An Ancient Portrait," the author portrays the struggle of the prophet Jonah to obey God's command.

Why did Jonah run when commanded to preach the gospel to the Ninevites and what was God's response?

After the storm came, what did the ship's crew finally decide to do with Jonah when they discovered it was his fault?

After sometime in the belly of the great fish, why did Jonah finally repent?

After Jonah finished preaching, what was God's final act to help Jonah recognize His compassion?

What contradiction in the Prophet Jonah's thinking led him to be hypocrite when it came to God's mercy?

Have you ever been in any situation comparable to Jonah's wicked perspective or the Ninevite's desperation? How was it different and how was it the same?

In the section, "A Modern Anecdote," the author describes a man angry and bitter against his father and how he learned to forgive him.

Why was the son so angry and bitter against his father?

How did the son demonstrate his bitterness?

Was the father a Christian, why or why not?

How did the believing son need to view his father in order to fully forgive him?

Since the father had passed away, how should the son finally decide to outwardly demonstrate his forgiveness?

Based on the truths learned in this chapter, what would you have done differently if you were the son who was neglected or the father who did the neglecting?

In the section, "A Personal Response," the author provides a model you may use for prayer if you find it necessary after discovering the truths in this chapter.

Are you presently in a relationship where you have sinned against another and have not asked God for forgiveness? If not, is there one from the past that still needs this prayer to be prayed?

Based on the truths you have just learned, what will you continue doing in your current relationships and what will you do differently?

What additional thoughts would you like to share with the others?

Chapter 4

Keep No Records

To fully forgive others means not only forgiving but also forgetting. We should not keep records of past offenses in order to punish others over and over.

In the section, "A Typical Scenario," the author describes a man's harshly reminding his wife of her past mistakes which will require a reconciliation.

What is the scenario about?

What did the conflict concern?

What was the relationship between the parties?

Have you had a similar experience?

In the section, "A Scriptural Principle" the author presents an important biblical principle in the forgiveness process which concerns forgiving and then forgetting the offenses.

How would you express this principle in your own words?

How would you rewrite this principle to make it even more personal to your life (using your name and situation)?

Why do you think this principle might be important in your life right now?

How would you rate yourself on the percentage of times you followed this principle in the past when you did something wrong in a relationship?

Directions: Put a horizontal mark and your name where you are on the percentage line.

0%	25%	50%	75%	100%

In the section, "A Biblical Explanation," the author explains the reasons why we should never keep records of the sins others have committed against us and how to do it.

What does the "churning" over and over others' sins against us result in?

When the Bible says "keep no records," what two things does it involve? What does it not involve?

What can happen to our relationships if we constantly bring up the sins of the past?

In 2 Corinthians 2:7, what was Paul's response when church members kept bringing up the repentant man's offense?

Does our Father, God, bring up our transgressions against Him over and over? Why or why not?

In what ways might these truths impact your relationships?

In the section, "An Ancient Portrait," the author describes the how Jesus did not hold Martha's previous sin against her when she confronted Him about allowing Lazarus to die.

What happened the first time Martha confronted the Lord?

After receiving a message from Martha, why did Jesus wait two more days before he began the journey to Lazarus?

When Martha chastised the Lord for not arriving in time, how did Jesus respond? How could He have?

When Mary took the same approach to Jesus as her sister, how did Jesus respond? How could He have responded?

Why didn't Jesus hold the previous confrontation against the sisters and refuse to resurrect Lazarus from the dead?

Have you ever been in a situation comparable to the Lord's second chastisement or Martha's constant confrontation? How was it different and how was it the same?

In the section, "A Modern Anecdote," the author shares the deep struggle of a daughter with her mother's reminders of her past mistakes.

What three transgressions of the daughter were on the list of her mother's mental records of sins against her?

How did the harsh reminders impact the daughter?

When the mother was gently confronted about what she had done, what was her initial reaction?

What was the mother's final response?

What was the next step the mother had to take after this final response?

Based on the truths learned in this chapter, what would you have done differently if you were the record-keeping mother or the discouraged daughter?

In the section, "A Personal Response," the author provides a model you may use for prayer if you find it necessary after discovering the truths in this chapter.

Are you presently in a relationship where you have sinned against another and have not asked God for forgiveness? If not, is there one from the past that still needs this prayer to be prayed?

Based on the truths you have just learned, what will you continue doing in your current relationships and what will you do differently?

What additional thoughts would you like to share with the others?

Chapter 5

Restore Through Action

Once our sins have been dealt with through forgiveness, we begin the restoration process. This will involve a change in our words and actions allowing the feelings to follow.

In the section, "A Typical Scenario," the author describes a broken relationship between a man and his mother which needed reconciliation.

What is the scenario about?

What did the conflict concern?

What was the relationship between the parties?

Have you had a similar experience?

In the section, "A Scriptural Principle" the author presents an important biblical principle in the forgiveness process which concerns the restoring of relationships through action.

How would you express this principle in your own words?

How would you rewrite this principle to make it even more personal to your life (using your name and situation)?

Why do you think this principle might be important in your life right now?

How would you rate yourself on the percentage of times you followed this principle in the past when you did something wrong in a relationship?

Directions: Put a horizontal mark and your name where you are on the percentage line.

| 0% | 25% | 50% | 75% | 100% |

In the section, "A Biblical Explanation," the author explains the reasons why we must restore the relationship through actions and how to do it.

What is the first step in mending a broken relationship?

In the second step of the mending process, what should we remind ourselves of?

In the third step of this process, what kind of actions should be taken?

As we mend the holes in our relationships, should we focus on our feelings? Why or why not?

According to Galatians 6:1, who should start the restoration process?

In what ways might these truths impact your relationships?

In the section, "An Ancient Portrait," the author describes Jacob's reconciliation with Esau.

What was the initial problem between Jacob and Esau which caused the rift in their relationship?

Why did Jacob have to finally face Esau? Do you think God was behind this and why?

What steps did Jacob take to reconcile with his brother?

How did Esau respond?

Did the brothers become close after this restoration? Why or why not?

Have you ever been in any situation comparable to Jacob's deceit or Esau's contempt and yet have to face the other person? How was it different and how was it the same?

In the section, "A Modern Anecdote," the author explains the difficulties a set of triplets were experiencing with each other and how they were able to reconcile.

How did these siblings handle their conflicts while growing up?

How did the mother respond?

When the triplets became adults, how did they handle the family interactions?

Why was it important for the children of the triplets to have their parents reconcile?

When did some feelings of love for one another finally begin to appear?

Based on the truths learned in this chapter, what would you have done differently if you were one of the triplets or the mother?

In the section, "A Personal Response," the author provides a model you may use for prayer if you find it necessary after discovering the truths in this chapter.

Are you presently in a relationship where you have sinned against another and have not asked God for forgiveness? If not, is there one from the past that still needs this prayer to be prayed?

Based on the truths you have just learned, what will you continue doing in your current relationships and what will you do differently?

What additional thoughts would you like to share with the others?

Conclusion

As we conclude this book, I would like to leave us with some final thoughts about our God of forgiveness and what His Son did on the cross for us. First, if we understand the full extent of what was wrought for us on that cursed tree in order to forgive us, it will become so much easier to do the same thing for others. Second, if you read this entire book and realized that you do not understand salvation or have never received Christ as Lord and Savior, then I would like to provide that opportunity. Please do not skip this section; it may be the most important in your life.

From all outward appearances, humans seem "good" and attempt to live decent lives. This is man's concept of himself. This is not God's concept. The Almighty's view is that people all over the world and throughout the ages sin, sin, and sin again (Romans 3:23). This is a terrible and utterly destructive condition. Yet, they have ramifications that are far worse. These sins condemn us to everlasting divine retribution.

Though described briefly in the Old Testament, the Lord Jesus Christ clearly announced and proclaimed the future punishment to come. Contrary to popular belief, Jesus did not only speak of love, grace, and mercy, He also spoke of the coming judgment for sin. He declared that the judgment of sin would be everlasting punishment in a place He called "Hell." The Lord portrayed this place as an eternal inferno (Matthew 18:8) where there would be the weeping (from the sorrow) and gnashing of teeth (from the agony and anguish of suffering) continually into eternity (Matthew 8:12; 13:42, 50; 22:13; 24:51; 25:30; Luke 13:28).

Why must people face this horrific punishment? Though God is a God of love, grace, and mercy, He is also a God of

33

great holiness, righteousness, and justice (Psalm 89:14,18). These attributes are just as much a part of His divine nature as His love, grace, and mercy. You have broken God's law as we all have and the penalty must be paid. This began with the first man Adam (Genesis 3:1-7). When this occurred, His love, grace, and mercy surfaced and a provision was made. Someone else would have to take man's place and pay the penalty. Someone who had never transgressed Him, who would never deserve punishment, and would fulfill all of God's Laws, would be substituted in man's place. This was the Son of God, Jesus Christ.

As the God-Man, He would pay the penalty for our sins in His death on the cross. Once done, the Lord God made only one provision for people to appropriate what His Son had done on the cross for them. This provision is receiving Jesus Christ as Savior and Lord. Though I cannot possibly share with you this good news in the confines of this book, I would love for you to consider purchasing my book entitled, *Finding The Light: The Kingdom of Heaven and How To Enter It.* It can be found for sale on Amazon.com. It is inexpensive and contains the full gospel message for your consideration. This message is so important and extensive that it cannot adequately be contained in a few pages at the end of a book.

If you are a believer, you must go out into the world and forgive as you are forgiven. These principles are to be lived and shared with others. You now have the tools to make your relationships last a lifetime. Go live them out and share them with others!

ABOUT THE AUTHOR

Dr. Donald Jones is currently a Christian Pastoral Counselor with thirty-eight years of experience in the fields of pastoral ministry, public education, and Christian counseling. He carries degrees and certificates from four major universities and from a variety of educational institutions. He has been a professor of Languages and Bible, a television commentator, and a featured speaker at a variety of events and seminars at churches, schools, and other organizations across the United States. He is a member in good standing of several secular and Christian professional organizations. Dr. Jones has been a published author since 1976. For further information view his website at www.donjonesphd.com.

www.ingramcontent.com/pod-product-compliance
Lightning Source LLC
Chambersburg PA
CBHW021120020426
42331CB00004B/564